A Kid's Guide to Drawing the Countries of the World™

How to Draw
Mexico's
Sights and Symbols

Melody S. Mis

The Rosen Publishing Group's
PowerKids Press™
New York

To Leonila Badger, who made Spanish class a joy

Published in 2003 by The Rosen Publishing Group, Inc.
29 East 21st Street, New York, NY 10010

First Edition

Editor: Jannell Khu
Book Design: Emily Muschinske

Illustration Credits: Emily Muschinske

Photo Credits: Cover and p. 22 © Tania Midgley/CORBIS; p. 5 © © Paul Almasy/CORBIS; p. 9 © Danny Lehman/CORBIS; p. 10 © Charles & Josette Lenars/CORBIS; pp. 12, 30 © Bettmann/CORBIS; p. 13 © (2004) Banco de México, Diego Rivera & Frida Kahlo Museum Trust. Av. Cinco de Mayo No. 2 Col. Centro, Del. Cuauhtémoc, México D.F.; Reproducción autorizada por el Instituto Nacional de Bellas Artes y Literatura; DIEGO RIVERA, Paisaje con cactus, 1931, óleo/tela, 125.5 x 150 cm, Col. Jaques y Natasha Gelman. México; p. 16 © Eyewire; p. 20 © Robin Chittenden; Frank Lane Picture Agency/CORBIS; pp. 24, 32 © Reuters New Media Inc./CORBIS; pp. 26, 38 © Randy Faris/CORBIS; p. 28 © Michael T. Sedam/CORBIS; p. 34 © Jonathan Blair/CORBIS; p. 36 © Buddy Mays/CORBIS; p. 40 © World Monuments Fund; p. 42 © Carl and Anne Purcell/CORBIS.

Mis, Melody S.
   How to draw Mexico's sights and symbols / Melody S. Mis.
     p. cm. — (A kid's guide to drawing the countries of the world)
   Summary: Presents step-by-step directions for drawing the flag, coat of arms, national bird, Aztec sunstone, Presidential Palace, and other sights and symbols of Mexico.
   Includes bibliographical references and index.
   ISBN 0-8239-6668-2 (library bdg.)
   1. Mexico—In art—Juvenile literature. 2. Drawing—Technique—Juvenile literature.   [1. Mexico—In art. 2. Drawing—Technique.]   I. Title. II. Series.
NC790.M57 2004
743'.93672—dc21

2002012667

Manufactured in the United States of America

CONTENTS

1	Let's Draw Mexico	4
2	More About Mexico	8
3	The Artist Diego Rivera	12
4	Map of Mexico	14
5	Flag of Mexico	16
6	Mexico's Coat of Arms	18
7	The Crested Caracara	20
8	The Dahlia	22
9	Day of the Dead Celebration	24
10	Teotihuacán	26
11	Chichén Itzá	28
12	The Aztecs	30
13	Popocatépetl and Iztaccíhuatl	32
14	Benito Juárez	34
15	La Parroquia	36
16	The National Palace	38
17	The Palace of Fine Arts	40
18	The Angel of Independence	42
	Timeline	44
	Mexico Facts	45
	Glossary	46
	Index	48
	Web Sites	48

Let's Draw Mexico

People from Asia followed herds of animals across what is known today as the Bering Strait and down through North America to Mexico 20,000 years ago. The animals were their source of food. By 8,000 B.C., the people learned to grow food and settled into villages. These villages developed into civilizations. The Olmec people established the first important civilization in the Gulf of Mexico around 1500 B.C. Some people consider the Olmecs to be the "mother culture," because they influenced a succession of civilizations in and around Mexico. The Olmecs built cities and carved beautiful stone statues. The Toltecs ruled central Mexico between 700 and 300 B.C. They built pyramids to honor their gods. Around A.D. 300–900, the Mayan Indians thrived in southern Mexico and Central America. The Maya used their advanced mathematical and astronomical knowledge to develop calendars.

Mexico is named for the Mexica peoples. They were a northern tribe that became part of the

Located in Tula, Mexico, these four stone sculptures are called the Atlantes. They guard the Toltec temple called Morning Star. The giant sculptures are 15 feet (4.5 m) tall.

Aztec nation. The Aztecs' rise to power began in the early 1300s. By 1428, they ruled central Mexico. In 1519, Spain sent explorer Hernán Cortés to Mexico to look for treasure. The Aztecs were frightened when they saw Cortés and his men. They had never seen white men or guns. The Aztec leader, Moctezuma II, thought Cortés was a god and offered him gold and silver. When Cortés saw these riches, he declared war on the Aztecs and defeated them in 1521. The Aztec Empire was Mexico's last great empire. After the Aztecs were defeated, Spain ruled Mexico for the next 300 years. The Aztec lands were given to Spanish noblemen. The Indians had to work for the noblemen and pay them taxes.

During the early 1800s, the Indians finally revolted against Spain. Father Miguel Hidalgo y Costilla is considered the father of Mexican independence. He was the first to call for rebellion against Spanish rule. Mexico won its independence from Spain in 1821.

In 1861, Benito Juárez became president. He worked to establish a democratic government. Revolutionary leaders began fighting for government reforms during the early 1900s. One of these leaders was Francisco Villa, known also as Pancho Villa. He took land from the wealthy people and gave it back to the Indians. After the Mexican Revolution (1910–1920), Mexico became a democratic country. In this book, you will learn more about Mexico and how to draw many of its sights and symbols. Directions are under each drawing. Each new step is shown in red. You will need the following supplies to draw Mexico's sights and symbols.

- A sketch pad
- An eraser

- A number 2 pencil
- A pencil sharpener

These are some of the shapes and drawing terms you need to know to draw Mexico's sights and symbols:

— Horizontal line

◯ Oval

▭ Rectangle

▰ Shading

〰 Squiggle

▱ Trapezoid

△ Triangle

| Vertical line

∿ Wavy line

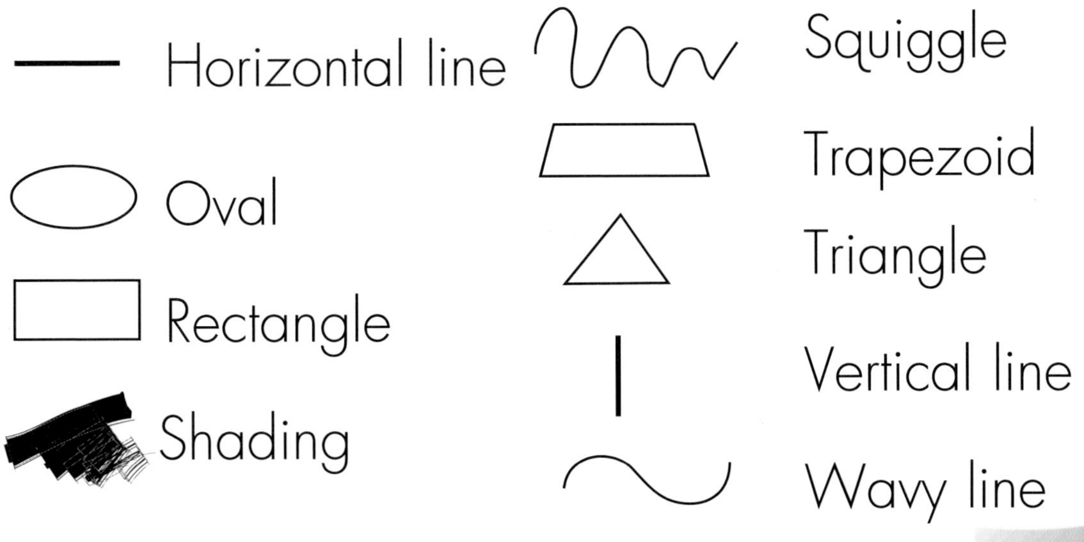

More About Mexico

Mexico is the second-most-populated country in Latin America with about 100 million residents. Of these residents, 60 percent are mestizos, and 30 percent are Indians. Mestizos are people with white and Indian ancestry. Nine percent of the population is of Spanish ancestry, and 1 percent is made up of other races.

Mexico City is the capital of Mexico. With a population of more than 18 million people, it is the second-most-populated city in the world. The capital is located 7,500 feet (2,286 m) above sea level and is surrounded by mountains. Many of the country's most important government buildings, businesses, schools, and museums are located in and around Mexico City.

Mexico's economy is based on manufacturing, agriculture, mining, and tourism. Mexico produces cars, processed foods, clothing, and steel. Its main agricultural products include coffee, corn, and sugarcane. Mexico is the world's leader in the production of silver. Other minerals found in

Mexico City is the second-most-populated city in the world, second to Tokyo, Japan. This is a view of Mexico City, which is surrounded by mountains.

Mexico include copper, gold, and oil. Tourism is important to Mexico's economy. Some of the world's most beautiful beaches and resorts are located in Acapulco, Mazatlán, and Cancún. Mexico's historical archaeological sites are also major tourist attractions.

Although Spanish is the official language of Mexico, some Indians still speak their own language. The two most commonly spoken Indian languages are Nahuatl and Maya. Nahuatl is spoken by more than one-fourth of the Indian population.

When Spain conquered Mexico, many Catholic missionaries were sent to convert the Indians to Catholicism. Although there is freedom of religion in Mexico, nearly 90 percent of the population is Roman Catholic. Mexico's government is similar to that of the United States. It is a federal republic, which means Mexico's states are united under a central government. The people of Mexico vote to elect their president and their representatives to various government offices.

Dancers in colorful costumes perform outside the Basílica of Guadalupe, located in Mexico City. A basilica is a type of church.

The Artist Diego Rivera

Diego Rivera (1886–1957) is considered one of Mexico's greatest artists. He was born in Guanajuato, Mexico, and studied classical art at the San Carlos Academy of Fine Arts in Mexico City. Classical art refers to the art of ancient Greece and Rome. In 1907, Rivera went to Europe to study the works of great

Diego Rivera

Spanish artists, such as Francisco de Goya, El Greco, and Pablo Picasso. Rivera especially admired Picasso, who started a new art movement called cubism. In cubism the artist's subject does not look realistic. Instead the subject is drawn in squares, cones, and circles. While Rivera was in Europe, he also studied fresco painting. Frescoes are paintings done on wet plaster walls. When Rivera returned to Mexico, he developed his own style of painting. Rivera wanted his paintings to represent the history of Mexico. He also wanted his work to be seen by as many people as possible, so he painted murals on the walls of buildings. Murals are large paintings on walls. Rivera's murals show Mexico's people, events, and social problems. Many of Rivera's murals are found in Mexico's important government buildings and museums.

In 1929, Rivera married Frida Kahlo (1907–1954). Kahlo was born in Coyoacán, Mexico. Kahlo is one of Mexico's beloved and famous artists. She taught herself to paint while she was recovering from injuries she had received in a bus accident. Kahlo painted many pictures of herself and her experiences, including her injuries. She became famous for her strange and colorful images.

Rivera's *Landscape with Cactus* was painted in 1931 and measures 49 ⅖" x 59" (125.5 x 150 cm). At first glance, the painting appears to be of a simple, quiet Mexican landscape. However, if you look closely, the cactus plants resemble people talking to one another! Diego painted each cactus in a different position to give the painting a sense of movement.

Map of Mexico

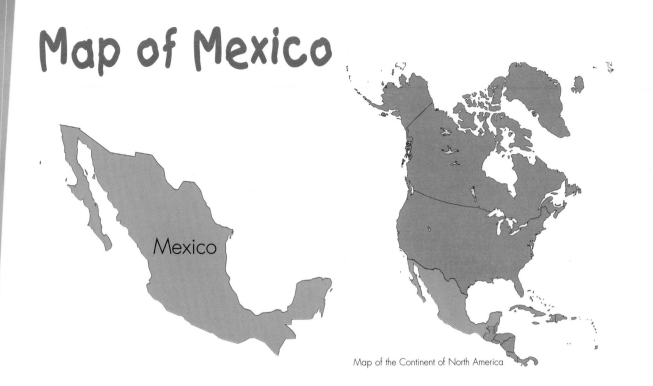

Mexico

Map of the Continent of North America

Mexico borders the United States to the north and Guatemala and Belize to the south. Mexico is between the Gulf of Mexico to the east and the Pacific Ocean to the west. Baja California in the northwest and the Yucatán in the southeast are Mexico's two peninsulas. Northwest Mexico is mostly mountainous desert country. The largest and most-populated area lies in the central plateau between two ranges of the Sierra Madre. This area is made up of volcanoes, flatlands, and canyons, including the Copper Canyon. Southern Mexico is marked by deep gorges, rain forests, and jungles. The highest mountain in Mexico is Pico de Orizaba. It rises 18,700 feet (5,699.8 m) above the central plateau.

1 Start with two triangle shapes. Notice the position and the size of the triangles. These shapes are guides to help you draw Mexico.

2 Draw the wavy line shown in red. You just drew Mexico's northern border, which separates the country from the United States.

3 Draw the peninsula of Baja California. A peninsula is an area of land surrounded by water on three sides. Baja California juts out into the Pacific Ocean.

4 Add the wavy, southwestern border. You are shaping the big triangle so that it looks like the country of Mexico.

5 Next draw a curved line that looks like a C. Be careful of the placement of this line. It extends through both triangles.

6 Copy the red line shown in the smaller triangle. Notice that the lines in this step connect to the lines that you drew in the bigger triangle.

7 Erase the triangle guides. You just finished drawing Mexico.

8 After you add some of Mexico's key places, you are finished! You can also draw the map key shown below.

☆ Mexico City

△ Chichén Itzá

○ Teotihuacán

▱ Popo and Izta

⌂ Baja California

Flag of Mexico

Mexico's original flag was adopted in 1821. The flag is tricolor with three wide, vertical stripes. The green stripe stood for independence, the center white stripe stood for the Catholic religion, and the red stripe stood for the union between Spain and Mexico. When Benito Juárez became president in 1858, he pushed for a democratic government and the separation of church and state. Under his presidency, the colors of the flag took on different meanings. Green stood for hope, white for purity and the unity of Mexico. Red stood for the blood of the nation's heroes. The coat of arms in the center stripe of the flag has been redesigned many times since it was first used in 1821. The design still used today was adopted in 1968, when Mexico was preparing to host the Olympic Games.

1

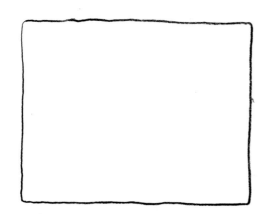

Begin by drawing a big rectangle for the flag field. The rectangle needs to be big enough to include Mexico's coat of arms, which you will learn to draw in the next chapter.

2

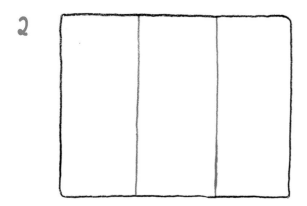

Draw two vertical lines. After you are done, you should have three rectangles of equal size.

3

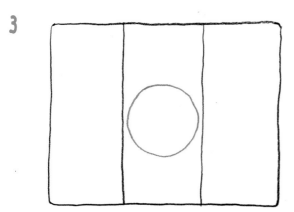

Draw a circle in the center rectangle. Make sure the circle is big enough for you to draw Mexico's coat of arms.

4

Shade the left and right rectangles. Or, if you'd like, you can color the left rectangle green and the right rectangle red.

5

To draw Mexico's coat of arms, follow the directions on page 19.

17

Mexico's Coat of Arms

Mexico's current coat of arms was adopted in 1968. According to an ancient Aztec legend, the gods told the Aztecs to build a city where they saw an eagle sitting on a cactus and eating a snake. The Aztecs found their eagle on an island in the middle of a lake. Around 1325, the Aztecs built their city and called it Tenochtitlán.

On the coat of arms is an eagle with a rattlesnake in its mouth. The eagle stands on a green cactus that grows from a rock surrounded by water. Beneath the cactus and the water is a half circle of leaves. A green, white, and red ribbon ties the two branches of leaves together. The colors of the ribbon are the national colors of Mexico.

1

Inside the circle you drew in step 3 of the previous chapter, draw an oval. Draw another oval inside the first one.

2

Use wavy lines to draw the basic shape of the eagle's body and wings. The shape on the left is the body. The shape on the right is the wings.

3

Draw the beak. Draw the details on the eagle's head. Draw the tail feathers using five lines of different lengths.

4

After you erase the extra lines, you will have the finished shape of the eagle's body and wings. Add its feet. The sharp, pointed parts of its claws are called talons. Use long, wavy lines to draw the snake in the eagle's beak.

5

Use teardrop shapes to draw the cactus.

6

Beneath the cactus draw a rectangular rock with wavy water around it. Add two branches curving around the eagle. The branch on the right has long leaves. The left branch has leaves that are more round.

7

In this step you will add details. Start with the cactus needles. Finish the branches. Add the eagle's eye and the lines for its feathers.

8

Shade your drawing.
Good job.

The Crested Caracara

The crested caracara is the national bird of Mexico. It is often called the Mexican eagle. Falcons are raptors, which means they hunt animals for food. The crested caracara is from 16 to 24 inches (40.6–61 cm) long. It has a wingspan of 48 inches (1.2 m). The top, or crest, of the bird's head is dark brown or black, depending on its age. The area around its beak is red. The caracara has a long white neck, a black body, and long yellow legs. Its tail is white

with black stripes. The caracara lives on the Mexican plains. It often rests in tall trees with other caracaras. From their perches, the birds can easily spot food, such as snakes and mice.

1

Begin with an egg shape. This is the bird's body.

2

Add the arch on top of the egg shape. This is a guide shape that will help you to draw the bird's neck and head.

3

For the tail, draw the shape shown beneath the bird's body.

4

Next let's shape the bird's neck and beak. Inside the arch you drew in step 2, draw the shape shown here.

5

Erase extra lines. Draw a curved line across the top of the bird's head. In the middle of this line, draw the eye. Draw a long, vertical, curved line as shown here for the wing.

6

Add two thin legs, and feet with pointy claws. Notice that the legs come out of small *U* shapes.

7

Erase the extra lines through the legs. Add the details to the beak. Notice the way the beak curls downward. Draw the perch.

8

Shade the drawing. Notice where the shading is dark and where it is light. You just drew Mexico's national bird, the caracara.

The Dahlia

Mexico's national flower is the dahlia. This flower is native to Mexico and Central America. The dahlia grows best in high altitudes and rocky areas. The dahlia reached Spain in the 1700s. Its beauty caused such excitement that the king of Spain named a day of celebration to honor the dahlia. He named the dahlia for Swedish botanist Anders Dahl.

Two types of dahlias include the anemone and the cactus. The anemone dahlia has rounded petals. The cactus dahlia has skinny, spiky petals. The colors of the dahlia range from white to bright orange. The Aztecs ate the dahlia's stem for food.

1

Begin by drawing the round center of the dahlia. Attach a petal. The petal is almond shaped.

2

Continue adding almond-shaped petals. Notice that the petals overlap.

3

Add two more petals.

4

Finish drawing the petals. You should have nine petals.

5

Add tiny circles inside the center of the flower.

6

Shade the center of the dahlia. If you look at the photo, you can see that the outer part of the flower's center is lighter than the inner part.

7

Shade the petals. Notice that the shading is darker toward the center. You just drew Mexico's national flower, the dahlia!

23

Day of the Dead Celebration

The Day of the Dead is held November 1–2 in Mexico to remember and honor family members who have passed away. The celebration is joyous. It is not a time of sadness. Families prepare for the Day of the Dead by making skeleton dolls and floral decorations for home altars and graves. They are gifts for deceased relatives. Families also decorate the altar with flowers, candles, and a photograph of the person who died. Mexicans believe the spirits of their deceased relatives will come home for a visit, so food is prepared for them.

On November 2, families gather at the cemetery. They clean and decorate the grave sites with flowers or crosses. Some families take a picnic lunch to the cemetery. Some families even spend the night there!

1

Begin by drawing a circle for the head. Add a triangle for the mouth.

2

Draw a long vertical line to use as a guide for the body. Add a stack of neck bones.

3

Add the basic shape of the rib cage. Notice that it looks like the letter D.

4

Erase the long guideline that you drew in step 2. Use a curved line for the front part of the jacket. Use L shapes to draw the arm. Add a collar to the jacket.

5

Outline the mouth and erase the extra lines. Draw the right side of the jacket.

6

Draw the raised right arm. Next draw the hands. Start from the wrist and draw each finger one at a time.

7

Draw teeth. Add a triangle nose and two eyes. Add horizontal lines for the skeleton's ribs. Add two curved lines to the head for detail.

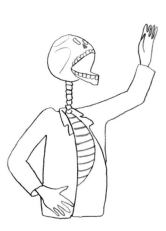

8

Add details and shading. Notice that the mouth and the inside of the jacket are very dark.

Teotihuacán

The Toltecs started to build their ancient city near what is now Mexico City around 200–150 B.C. The Toltecs named the city Teotihuacán, which means "city of the gods." Teotihuacán was the most powerful city in Mexico for about 500 years. At the peak of its power, Teotihuacán housed from 125,000 to 200,000 people and covered more than 8 square miles (20.7 sq km). The Toltecs built temples, palaces, and pyramids in Teotihuacán. One of the most famous landmarks in Teotihuacán is the Pyramid of the Sun. This pyramid was made from mud bricks and was covered with gravel and stone. The height of the Pyramid of the Sun is 213 feet (65 m). It is one of the tallest pyramids in the world.

1

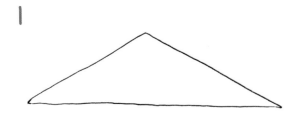

Draw a triangle.

2

Add a diagonal line toward the left side of the triangle.

3

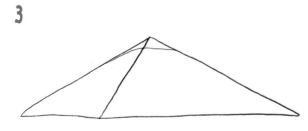

Soften the top of the pyramid by drawing a slightly curved horizontal line.

4

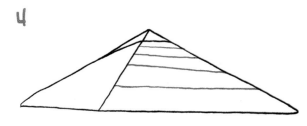

Draw four horizontal lines on the right side of the pyramid.

5

Add four lines on the left side of the pyramid. They should meet the ones you drew on the right.

6

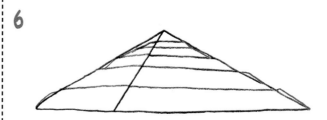

Notice that the sides of the pyramid are like large, worn steps. Add the bumps to make each layer look like a step.

7

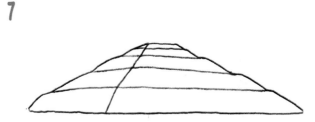

Erase extra lines.

8

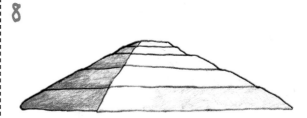

Shade the drawing. Notice that the left side of the pyramid is darker.

27

Chichén Itzá

Deep within the jungles of the Yucatán lies Chichén Itzá, one of the most impressive archaeological sites of the Mayan civilization. Chichén Itzá was the largest and most powerful Mayan city. At Chichén Itzá, the Maya built pyramids, ceremonial centers, and even a huge court where ball games were held. One of the most unusual buildings in the city is a pyramid called El Castillo, which means "the castle." When the sun set during certain times of the year, the shadow that the sun cast on the pyramid looked like a snake slithering down the steps! Today you can climb to the top of El Castillo and see the breathtaking view of Chichén Itzá below.

1

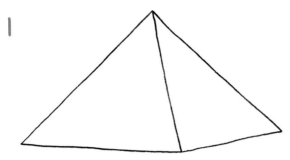

Begin by drawing two triangles that meet at the top point and share one side. You just drew a pyramid.

2

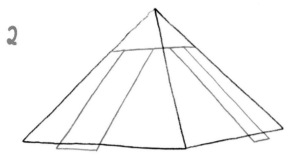

Draw a horizontal line near the top of the pyramid. Add two long rectangles on each side of the pyramid. Notice that these shapes stick out slightly past the bottom of the pyramid.

3

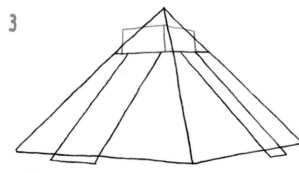

Add two rectangles to the top of the pyramid.

4

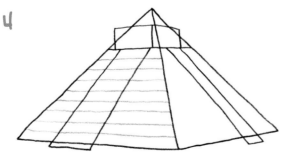

Draw horizontal lines across the left side of the pyramid.

5

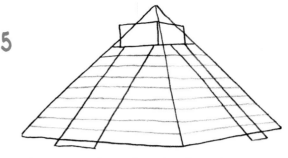

On the pyramid's right side, draw horizontal lines that meet the ones you just drew.

6

Add details inside the rectangle on top of the pyramid. Draw the pyramid steps.

7

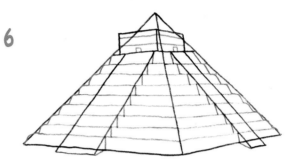

After you erase your extra lines, your pyramid should look like the above picture.

8

Shade your drawing and add detail. Shade the right side of the pyramid darker than the left side.

The Aztecs

The Aztecs ruled Mexico's last great civilization. The Aztecs were mighty warriors. By the 1420s, they ruled central Mexico. The Aztecs were violent people who offered captives as sacrifices to their gods. Neighboring tribes disliked the Aztecs and helped Cortés to defeat them. The Aztec Empire fell when the Spanish captured Tenochtitlán in 1521. The Aztecs advanced agriculture in Mexico by developing irrigated fields. They are also famous for their calendar, called a sunstone. The sunstone shows the 20 days of each Aztec month. Each day symbolizes something important to the Aztecs, such as rain, dogs, or flowers. The sun god sticks out his tongue in the center of the sunstone. On his tongue is a knife, which stands for the Aztec belief in blood sacrifices.

1

We'll simplify the drawing of the Aztec sunstone to focus on the basic shapes. Draw six circles, one inside another. Make sure you make them large enough to fit in all the details that will come later.

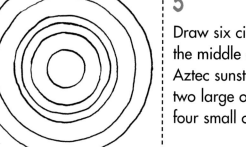

2

In the outermost space, draw short, straight lines. Add two triangles at the top of the circle.

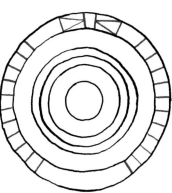

3

Add two short vertical lines next to the triangles. Add seven triangle shapes. Add curly tails to three of them. Draw an eighth triangle above the innermost circle.

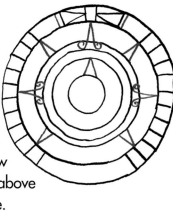

4

Add more straight lines in the center area of the circle. Then add the square shapes around the center.

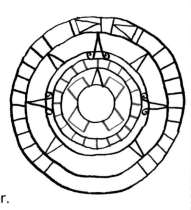

5

Draw six circles in the middle of the Aztec sunstone, two large ones and four small ones.

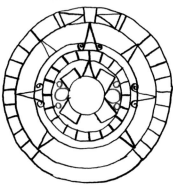

6

Add the shapes beside the top triangle of the Aztec sunstone. Next use long curled lines to create the fancy shapes at the bottom. First study the lines and then draw one line at a time.

7

Draw the face in the center. Draw one facial feature at a time.

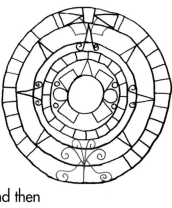

8

Make each line a double line. The second set of lines will make the Aztec sunstone look more like the real thing. Add as much detail as you like.

Popocatépetl and Iztaccíhuatl

About 45 miles (72.4 km) southeast of Mexico City, there are two famous mountains. The Aztecs named them Popocatépetl and Iztaccíhuatl. The mountains are actually volcanoes. They are nicknamed Popo and Izta. Popocatépetl means "smoking mountain." Popo often erupted ash into the sky, causing the area to look smoky. Iztaccíhuatl is called "sleeping lady," because its shape looks like a lady sleeping on her back. Popo is 17,887 feet (5,452 m) high. Izta is 17,343 feet (5,286.1 m) high. This makes them Mexico's second- and third-highest mountains.

Scientists have found artifacts from the mountains that suggest the Aztecs performed religious ceremonies on them. Today there are routes that climbers can take to the top of both Popo and Izta.

1

You will draw Popo shooting out ash. Begin with a triangle.

2

Add a smaller triangle on the right. These triangles will be your guides as you draw the mountain.

3

To shape the mountain peak, draw the wavy line as shown.

4

Soften the pointy peak on the smaller triangle.

5

Erase your guides. Add the small line shown above. Check to see if your drawing matches the photograph of Popo on the opposite page.

6

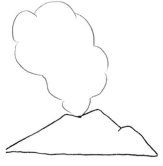

Draw the ash coming out of Popo. It doesn't have to be an exact shape, so have fun drawing! Notice that the ash looks like a fluffy cloud.

7

Add details so that the ash looks like the ash in the photograph.

8

Shade your drawing.

33

Benito Juárez

Benito Juárez (1806–1872) is a national hero in Mexico. There are many statues in Mexico that honor him, including the statue featured here. It stands in Oaxaca, his birthplace. Juárez was

orphaned when he was three. His uncle raised him. Juárez studied law and eventually became governor of Oaxaca. He also joined a liberal group that tried to establish a democratic government for Mexico. Juárez served as Mexico's president from 1861 to 1863 and from 1867 to 1872. During his presidencies, Juárez brought about many reforms. He decreased the power of the Catholic Church and gave some of the Church's land to the poor. He also enforced the constitution of 1857, which gave Mexicans important rights such as free speech and a free press.

1

First draw the base of the statue. Draw three lines, one horizontal and two slanted vertical lines. On top of this shape, draw a thin rectangle.

2

Draw two rectangles for Juárez's pants. Draw two curved lines for Juárez's shoe.

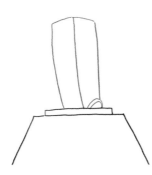

3

Draw Juárez's body using straight and curved lines. Study the drawing. First draw the left side. Then draw the middle part. Last draw the right side of his body. Add the buttons and collar.

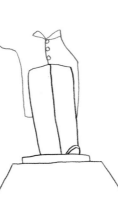

4

Draw the top of his raised arm. Then add swooping, curved lines to create the folds of Juárez's cape. Notice the way the fabric falls around his shoulders.

5

Add the rest of his cape using long, curved lines.

6

Add Juárez's hands. His raised hand is pointed. His left hand holds a book. For the book, draw a square and a rectangle.

7

Next draw Juárez's head. Add the features of his face.

8

Shade your drawing. Write "JUAREZ" on the base of the platform.

La Parroquia

San Miguel de Allende is a city located in central Mexico. Spanish colonists settled there after the Aztecs were defeated. The city was named in honor of General Ignacio Allende. When General Allende heard Father Hidalgo's cry for independence, he joined the rebel forces and led Mexico to several victories over Spain. One of the city's most famous landmarks is a church called La Parroquia, which means "parish church." Local architect Zeferino Gutiérrez remodeled the church in the late nineteenth century. Two architectural styles used in La Parroquia are pointed arches and ribbed vaulting. Ribbed vaulting refers to arched ceilings made of stone with decorative carvings on the underside of the ceilings.

1

This church is drawn with a few basic shapes, shown above. From left to right, we've named them fluted column, triangle, arched entrance, pointed column, and oval. If you practice these shapes, you will have an easy time drawing the church.

2

Draw two sets of two fluted columns, one on top of the other. Add two triangles to the upper fluted columns. Draw a slanted rectangle to create the basic shape of the building.

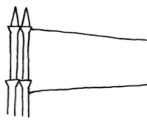

3

Draw several triangles. These will become the church towers. Add a vertical line.

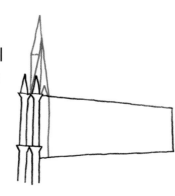

4

Add arched entrances and lines inside the slanted rectangle. Notice how many vertical lines the building has. Remember to draw one shape at a time. Start drawing the shapes from left to right.

5 Add the triangles on top of the building.

6 Draw pointed columns on the top left side of the church. Draw them close together.

7 Add the tower behind the pointed columns. Draw the cross on top of the tower. Draw three small ovals inside this tower. Draw a smaller tower on the right.

8

Shade your church and you are done!

37

The National Palace

The National Palace houses government offices. The palace was built in 1529, on the site where Moctezuma II's palace once stood. After the building burned down in 1692, it was rebuilt and changed over the years. The palace covers two city blocks. It faces the eastern side of Mexico's public square, which is one of the largest city squares in the world. The palace was built in the baroque style. This architectural style is usually grand and has fancy decorations. The front of the palace is made of gray stone and red *tezontle*, which is a volcanic rock. Inside the palace, murals by Diego Rivera record Mexico's history. Father Hidalgo's Liberty Bell, which signaled Mexico's war for independence, hangs over the main balcony.

1

Let's focus on the center section of this wide building. Begin by drawing a rectangle. Erase a section at the top.

2

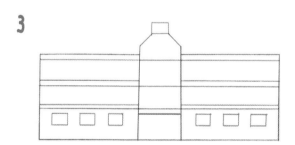

Draw a vertical rectangle. Then remove the top corners of it. Add four horizontal lines across the center.

3

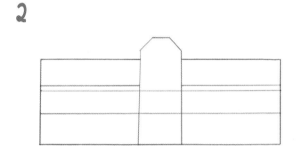

Add more lines across the building. Add seven rectangles.

4

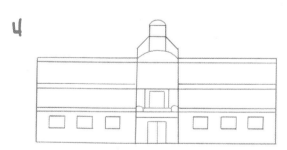

Starting at the bottom and working your way up, add two rectangles for a double door, two round shapes, two squares, a large arch, two more vertical lines, and a small arch at the top.

5

Add a line to the top. Then draw an oval window, a window made with two arches, two thin, vertical windows, and small circles for decoration.

6

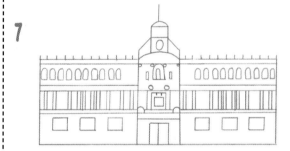

Add many vertical lines for columns. Add two tiny lines in the center window area.

7

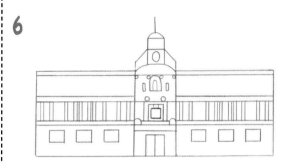

Draw short lines on top of the building. Then draw arched windows.

8

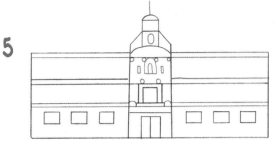

Shade your drawing. Erase the outside edges of the building to show that the building is wider than the portion you drew.

The Palace of Fine Arts

   The Palace of Fine Arts is one of the most beautiful buildings in Mexico City. It was built in the art nouveau style between 1904 and 1934. Art nouveau architecture is very decorative, with arches, curved lines, and fancy sculptures. The palace is made of Italian marble. Unfortunately, the weight of the building has caused one side of the building to sink about 9 feet (2.7 m) into the soft soil below. Inside the palace there is a glass curtain that is etched with scenes of the two volcanoes Popocatépetl and Iztaccíhuatl. Murals by Diego Rivera are also displayed on the palace walls. The huge auditorium of the palace is the home of the internationally famous Ballet Folklórico. This ballet company performs dances that show the history of Mexico's different cultures.

The Palace of Fine Arts is a project of the World Monuments Fund.
photo © World Monuments Fund

1

Draw two arches, one inside the other. Add a rectangle below them. Make the outside edges of the rectangle turn downward.

2

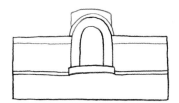

Draw a rectangle around the arches. Draw four horizontal lines in the center of the rectangle you just drew.

3

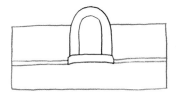

Draw two horizontal lines near the top of the rectangle. Add another arch above the first arches. Draw the shape shown above the last arch you drew.

4

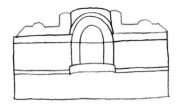

Follow the top edge of the building. Use a combination of lines that are diagonal, horizontal, curved, and vertical. Add a horizontal line across the arch.

5

Draw a large dome using a curved line. Next draw the small shape on top of the dome. Add arched windows.

6

Draw vertical lines topped with small half circles. These are the columns that support and decorate the building.

7

Draw long, rectangular windows and small, square windows.

8

Shade your drawing. Add details such as the curved lines of the dome.

41

The Angel of Independence

The Angel of Independence was erected in 1910. The monument consists of a column almost 164 feet (50 m) high with a sculpture of an angel on top. It honors the Mexican heroes who fought against

Spanish rule. During the late eighteenth century, Spain tried to gain more control over Mexico. This made many Mexicans angry, and they revolted. Father Hidalgo began the revolution for independence in 1810. He failed and was killed. Father Morelos y Pavón continued the fight and captured most of Mexico southwest of Mexico City from Spain. He too was killed. As the fight for independence grew stronger, Mexicans banded together and finally defeated Spain. In 1821, the Treaty of Córdoba gave Mexico its independence!

1

Begin with an oval for the head. Draw the front of the angel using curved lines.

2

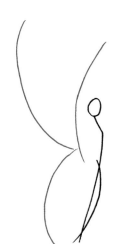

Draw three more curved lines.

3

Add a wavy line to create the top of the angel's wing. Draw the arm and hand, using the second curved line as your guide.

4

Add curved lines to create the large feathers. Erase extra lines.

5

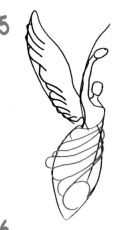

Use more curved lines to create the robe. Notice the way the robe blows out behind the angel.

6

Draw her leg and her foot.

7

Draw the base of the sculpture. Then add details to her hand. She is holding a wreath. Add her face and hair.

8

Add shading. Look at the picture to see which areas of the angel are the darkest. Give these areas of your drawing a dark shadow.

43

Timeline

20,000 B.C.	People from Asia arrive in Mexico.
1500–400 B.C.	Olmec Indians build the first major civilization in Mexico.
Around 200–150 B.C.	Toltec Indians build Teotihuacán.
A.D. 300–900	The Maya rule the Yucatán Peninsula.
1325	Aztecs found Tenochtitlán.
1502–1521	Moctezuma II is leader of the Aztecs.
1521	Cortés defeats the Aztecs.
1521–1821	Spain colonizes and governs Mexico.
1810	Father Hidalgo revolts against Spain for Mexico's independence.
1821	Mexico gains independence from Spain.
1846–1848	The Mexican-American War takes place.
1853	The United States gains territory from Mexico through the Gadsden Purchase.
1861–1863	Benito Juárez is president of Mexico.
1862–1867	France invades Mexico.
1867–1872	Benito Juárez defeats the French and becomes president again.
1876–1911	Porfirio Díaz is dictator.
1910–1920	Mexican Revolution is fought for government reforms.
1992	Mexico, Canada, and the United States sign NAFTA.

Mexico Facts

Official Name	United Mexican States
Area	759,530 square miles (1,967,173 sq km)
Population	99 million
Capital	Mexico City, population, 19 million
Most Populated City	Mexico City
Industries	Cars, clothing, oil products, processed foods, textiles, steel
Agriculture	Corn, sugarcane, coffee, cotton, avocados
National Flower	Dahlia
National Bird	Crested caracara
National Dance	Mexican hat dance
National Sport	*Charrería*, similar to a rodeo
National Anthem	"National Anthem of Mexico"
Language	Spanish
Highest Mountain Peak	Pico de Orizaba, 18,700 feet (5,700 m)
Longest River	Rio Grande, 1,885 miles (3,033 km)
National Holidays	Constitution Day, February 5, Cinco de Mayo, May 5, Independence Day, September 16, Revolution Day, November 20

Glossary

altitudes (AL-tih-toodz) Heights above Earth's surface.

ancestry (AN-ses-tree) Having to do with a person's relatives who lived long ago.

archaeological (ar-kee-uh-LAH-jih-kul) Having to do with the study of the way humans lived a long time ago.

architect (AR-kih-tekt) Someone who designs a building.

artifacts (AR-tih-fakts) Objects created and produced by humans.

astronomical (a-struh-NAH-mih-kul) Having to do with the science of the Sun, the Moon, the planets, and the stars.

botanist (BAH-tun-est) A person who studies flowers.

canyons (KAN-yunz) Deep, narrow valleys.

cemetery (SEH-muh-ter-ee) A place where the dead are buried.

ceremonial (ser-ih-MOH-nee-ul) Having to do with a ceremony, or a series of actions done for a special occasion.

coat of arms (KOHT UV ARMZ) A design on and around a shield or on a drawing of a shield.

constitution (kon-stih-TOO-shun) The basic rules by which a country or a state is governed.

convert (kun-VERT) To change from one religious belief to another.

culture (KUL-chur) The beliefs, practices, and arts of a group of people.

democratic (deh-muh-KRA-tik) In favor of democracy, a system in which people choose their leaders.

developed (dih-VEH-lupt) To have worked out in great detail.

empire (EM-pyr) A large area under one ruler.

etched (EHCHT) Carved with designs.

gorges (GORJ-ez) Steep, narrow passages through land.

grave sites (GRAYV SYTS) Places where dead people are buried.

impressive (im-PREH-siv) Having a strong effect on the mind or feelings.

independence (in-dih-PEN-dents) Freedom or self-rule.

injuries (IN-juh-reez) Physical harm or damages to a person.

irrigated (EER-ih-gayt-ed) To supply land with water through ditches or pipes.

legend (LEH-jend) A story, passed down through the years, that cannot be proven.

liberal (LIH-buh-rul) Favoring political progress and reforms, or changes.

missionaries (MIH-shuh-ner-eez) People who are sent to do religious work in a foreign country.

NAFTA (NAF-tuh) The North American Free Trade Agreement.

noblemen (NOH-bul-men) Members of royalty or other high-ranking people in a kingdom.

orphaned (OR-fund) No longer having parents.

peninsulas (peh-NIN-suh-luz) Areas of land surrounded by water on three sides.

plateau (pla-TOH) A broad, flat, high piece of land.

pyramids (PEER-uh-midz) Large, stone structures with square bottoms and triangular sides that meet in a point on top.

rebellion (ruh-BEL-yun) A fight against one's government.

reforms (rih-FORMZ) Changes or improvements.

representatives (reh-prih-ZEN-tuh-tivz) People chosen to speak for others.

revolted (rih-VOLT-ed) To have fought back.

revolutionary (reh-vuh-LOO-shuh-ner-ee) New or very different.

sacrifices (SA-krih-fys-ez) Things that have been given up or killed for a belief.

succession (suk-SEH-shun) Persons or things following one after another.

symbolizes (SIM-buh-lyz-ez) Stands for something else.

thrived (THRYVD) To have been successful; to have done well.

tourism (TUR-ih-zem) A business that deals with people who travel for pleasure

violent (VY-lent) Strong, rough force.

Index

A

Acapulco, Mexico, 11, 42
Allende, General Ignacio, 36
Aztecs, the, 6, 18, 22, 30, 32, 36

C

Cancún, Mexico, 11
Chichén Itzá, 28
Cortés, Hernán, 6, 30

E

El Castillo, 28

G

Gulf of Mexico, 4, 14

H

Hidalgo y Costilla, Miguel, 6, 36, 38, 42

I

Iztaccíhuatl, 32, 40

J

Juárez, Benito, 6, 34

L

La Parroquia, 36

M

Maya, the, 4, 28
Mazatlán, Mexico, 11
Mexica, the, 4
Mexican Revolution, 7
Mexico City, Mexico, 8, 26, 32, 40
Moctezuma II, 6, 38
Morelos y Pavón, Father José María, 42

N

Nahuatl, 11

O

Olmecs, the, 4

P

Palace of Fine Arts, the, 40
Pico de Orizaba, 14
Popocatépetl, 32, 40

R

Rivera, Diego, 12–13, 38, 40

S

Sierra Madre, 14
Spain, 6, 16, 42

T

Toltecs, the, 4, 26

V

Villa, Pancho, 7

Web Sites

Due to the changing nature of Internet links, PowerKids Press has developed an online list of Web sites related to the subject of this book. This site is updated regularly. Please use this link to access the list:
www.powerkidslinks.com/kgdc/mexico/